I Wonder What It's Like to Be an Earthworm

Erin M. Hovanec

The Rosen Publishing Group's
PowerKids Press™
New York

Published in 2000 by The Rosen Publishing Group, Inc.
29 East 21st Street, New York, NY 10010

Photo Credits: p. 4 © CORBIS/Robert Pickett, © Ed Reschke/Peter Arnold, Inc., © F.P.G./Luis Rosendo; p. 7 © CORBIS/Eric and David Hosking; p.8 © CORBIS/Science Pictures Limited; p. 10, 11, 12, 16 © Hans Pfletschinger/Peter Arnold, Inc.; p. 15 © S. J. Krasemann/Peter Arnold, Inc.; p. 19 © CORBIS/Joe McDonald, © CORBIS/Lynda Richardson, © CORBIS/Steve Austin Papillo; p. 20 © Manfred Danegger/Peter Arnold, Inc.; p. 22 © CORBIS/Robert Pickett

Photo Illustrations by Thaddeus Harden

First Edition

Book Design: Felicity Erwin

Hovanec, Erin M.
    I wonder what it's like to be an earthworm / by Erin Hovanec.
       p.   cm. — (Life science wonder series)
    Summary: Introduces the physical characteristics, habits, and behavior of earthworms.
    ISBN 0-8239-5454-4
    1. Earthworms Juvenile literature.   [Earthworms.] I. Title. II. Series: Hovanec, Erin M. Life science wonder series.
  QL391.A6H68 1999
  592'.64—dc21

99-29648
CIP

Manufactured in the United States of America

Contents

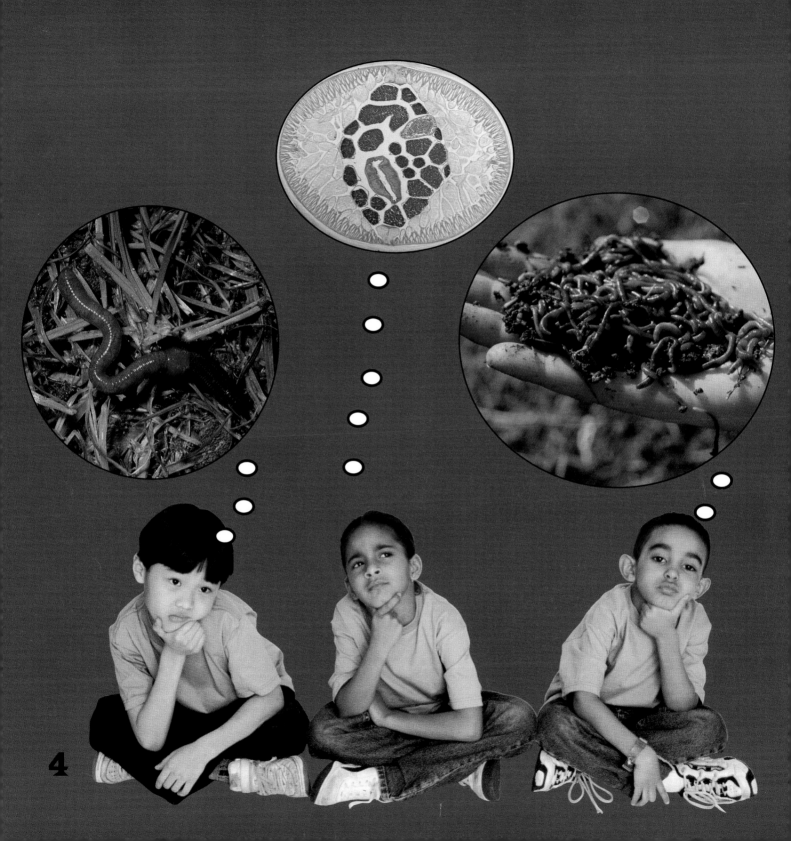

Worming Their Way Around

Earthworms may not look like much as they slither around on the ground, but earthworms are actually very complicated. Did you know that earthworms have five hearts, instead of just one? Did you know that they can grow new body parts if they get hurt?

Earthworms have a hidden life far below the surface of the earth. You may not see them very often, but they're there. Earthworms are just about everywhere. Have you ever wondered what it's like to be an earthworm?

◀ *There's a lot about earthworms you probably don't know.*

What's an Earthworm?

"Earthworm" is the name for many kinds of worms that live in the dirt. Most earthworms are a reddish-brown color. They have five hearts that work together to carry blood through their long bodies. Earthworms' bodies look smooth and shiny even though they are divided into **segments**. Earthworms can have more than 100 segments in their bodies. Some earthworms are so tiny that you can barely see them. Others are very long—sometimes 12 feet long. Can you imagine seeing an earthworm as long as a car?

A really long earthworm might ▶ even be longer than you!

7

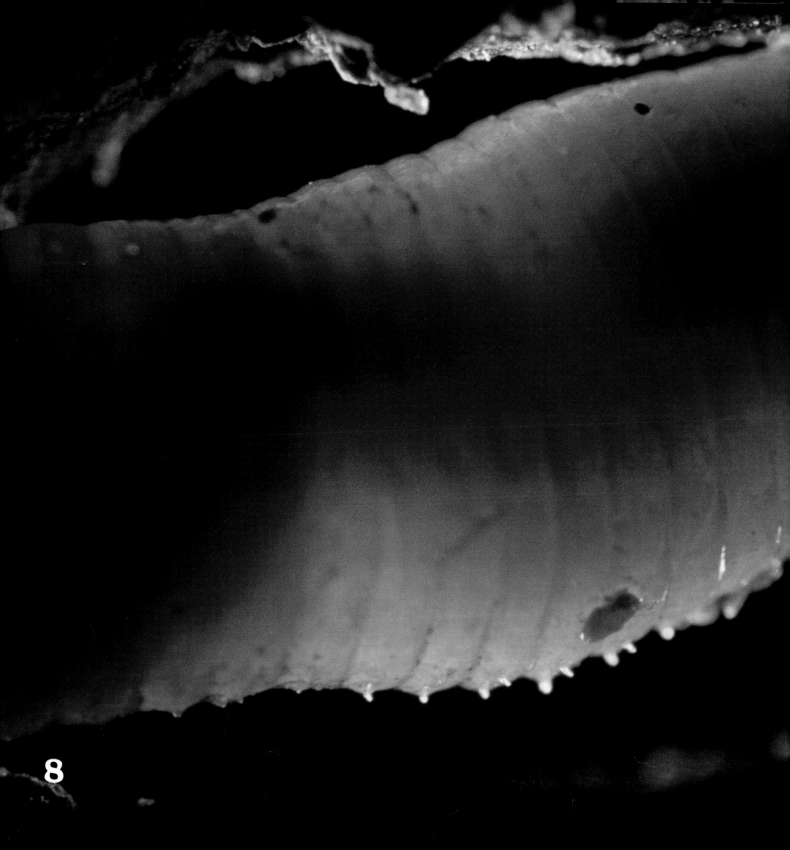

8

Light and Movement

Earthworms can't see, but they can **sense** light. They have special **cells** on their bodies that know whether it's light or dark. Earthworms can't hear, either. Instead, they can sense **vibrations**, or very tiny movements. An earthworm knows when an animal is moving nearby, because it can feel the animal's movements through the soil. Earthworms can also feel heat and cold.

How would you know where to go if you couldn't use your eyes to see, your ears to hear, and your hands to touch?

◀ *Earthworms sense light and sound with their bodies. They use these sensations to move around underground.*

Sliding Through the Soil

How would you get around without your legs to move you? Since earthworms don't have legs, they have special **muscles** to help them move. These muscles circle the worm's body and run along its sides. An earthworm has to push the front of its body through the soil and then pull its rear up to meet it. Earthworms also have hairy bristles called **setae** underneath their bodies to help them move. These bristles grab onto the soil and keep the worms from slipping.

◀ *Setae are hairy bristles that help earthworms move through the soil.*

This earthworm is using its muscles ▶
to push itself out of the ground.

Inside the Earth

Earthworms love cool, dark places. They don't like heat and sun at all. That's why they live underground. Earthworms **burrow**, or crawl, through the dirt looking for food. They usually stay near the surface of the soil.

Sometimes earthworms come above ground at night to eat. They also crawl to the surface when it rains because the rain fills their underground tunnels with water. Since earthworms **breathe** through their skin, they have to come to the surface for air. One kind of earthworm even climbs trees to keep from drowning!

A hole in the ground may not sound like home to you, but it's perfect for an earthworm.

◀ *Earthworms have to come up to the surface for air, but most of the time they're happier underground.*

Dirt Tastes Good

Earthworms eat dirt, and lots of it. In one day, the amount of food they eat often weighs as much as their own bodies!

As an earthworm travels through the soil, it eats as much dirt as it can. The dirt is filled with tiny parts of dead plants and sometimes dead animals. These contain yummy bits of **nutrients** that give the earthworm energy. Hungry earthworms can travel easily through the soil. They eat their way through the ground, making a tunnel for themselves to slide through!

Earthworms also eat leaves. They can open their mouths very wide to fit the leaves inside.

Not only does dirt give earthworms shelter from the sun, ▶
it gives them all the nutrients they need to live.

15

The Littlest Farmers

Earthworms are some of the best farmers around. They help plants grow all over the world.

After earthworms eat, their bodies get rid of waste material. This waste, called **castings**, makes the soil richer. It **fertilizes** the dirt with nutrients that plants need to grow and stay healthy.

Earthworms also bring air and water into the soil. They dig tiny tunnels in the ground through which air and rainwater can travel. Plants suck up air and water through their roots to stay alive. Earthworms work with nature to help plants grow.

◀ *If you were an earthworm, you'd help plants grow by fertilizing them and making it easier for them to get air and water.*

17

Earthworm Enemies

If you've ever gone fishing, you probably know that fish think earthworms are pretty tasty. Well, fish aren't the only ones. Earthworms have lots of **predators**. Predators are animals that live by eating or attacking other animals. Birds, frogs, moles, snakes, toads, and turtles all love to eat earthworms. Earthworms are almost three-quarters **protein**. All animals need protein to live. Earthworms are some animals' most important **prey**. Prey are animals that are eaten or attacked by other animals. Without earthworms to eat, many animals might starve!

Imagine if you were someone's favorite snack. ▶

Frogs...

newts...

...and leeches all
like to eat
earthworms.

19

20

An Awesome Ability

If you've ever fallen from your bike, you know that bumps and bruises can take a long time to heal. It takes time for our bodies to fix themselves after we've been hurt. Earthworms have a very special ability. When they get hurt, they grow new body parts to replace the injured ones.

Earthworms can **regenerate**, or replace, up to half of their bodies at a time. Sometimes part of an earthworm's body will get ripped off, like when a bird is pulling it out of the dirt. If this happens, the earthworm just grows a new part to replace the old one. The earthworm can grow a few segments, or even a new head or tail.

◀ *Birds sometimes injure the earthworms when they try to pull them out of the ground.*

Earthworms Are Amazing!

Earthworms live all over the world. Anywhere the soil contains enough food and water, you can find earthworms. Different people call earthworms by different names. Some are called fishworms or angleworms because they're used as fishing bait. Others call them night crawlers because they've seen the worms crawl to the soil's surface late at night. No matter what people call them, earthworms are amazing creatures. It might be neat to be an earthworm.

Glossary

breathe (BREETH) To take air in and out of one's body.

burrow (BUR-oh) To dig.

castings (KAST-ingz) Waste material from an earthworm's body.

cells (SELZ) The extremely small units of matter of which all living things are made.

fertilizes (FUR-tih-ly-zez) Gives a plant something that will help it grow.

muscles (MUH-suhlz) Body parts that help animals move.

nutrients (NOO-tree-ints) Things the body needs to live and grow.

predators (PREH-duh-turz) Animals that live by eating or attacking other animals.

prey (PRAY) An animal that is eaten or attacked by other animals.

protein (PRO-teen) A specific substance that plants and animals need to live.

regenerate (ree-JEHN-nuh-RAYT) To grow again.

segments (SEG-ments) Parts of a whole.

sense (SENS) To be aware of something.

setae (SEE-tee) Hairy bristles on the underside of an earthworm's body.

vibrations (vy-BRAY-shunz) Tiny movements.

Index

Web Sites:

You can learn more about earthworms on the Internet. Check out this Web site:

http://www.yucky.com/worm/